THE OFFICIAL TOTTENHAM HOTSPUR ANNUAL 2017

Written by Michael Bridge
Designed by B. Scott-Peterson

A Grange Publication

©2016. Published by Grange Communications Ltd., Edinburgh, under licence from Tottenham Hotspur Ltd. Printed in the EU.

Photographs © Action Images

ISBN 978-1-911287-15-5

CONTENTS

5   Welcome

6   Premier League Review

12 2015/2016 Season Stats

13 Capital One Cup Review

14 Europa League Review

16 Emirates FA Cup Review

18 Harry Kane – He's One of our Own

20 Spotlight: Toby Alderweireld

21 Spotlight: Dele Alli

22 Mauricio Pochettino – He's Magic, You Know…

24 Player Profiles

32 White Hot Moments

36 Spotlight: Victor Wanyama

37 Wordsearch

38 Spotlight: Vincent Janssen

39 New Signing

41 Spurs at Wembley!

42 International Spurs

44 Spurs Legends

46 Rising Stars

48 Super Spurs Quiz

50 Tottenham Pre-Season Report

52 I Love Eric Dier, Eric Dier Loves Me

54 Goal of the Season 2015/2016

56 Guess the Player

60 Quiz and Puzzle Answers

Dear Supporters,

Welcome to the 2017 Official Tottenham Hotspur Annual.

We finished 3rd in the Premier League last season, securing UEFA Champions League football.

It will certainly be a campaign to remember with an exciting run in the title race. On reflection, we achieved so much and are looking forward to doing it all again. After just missing out on the title, it made the squad determined to push on for further success.

Under Mauricio Pochettino, we now have a squad with a perfect blend of youth and experience. We were proud to see five members of our Club start for England at Euro 2016. Harry Kane won the Premier League Golden Boot award and Dele Alli, in his first season in the Premier League, won the PFA Young Player of the Year award. Congratulations to them both.

The Club is continuing to build on and off the pitch. As you approach White Hart Lane, you'll see our magnificent new stadium under construction.

Thank for your continued support.

Enjoy your new Annual.

Come on you Spurs!

Michael Bridge

2015/2016 WAS OUR BEST EVER SEASON IN THE PREMIER LEAGUE

We finished third in the table to guarantee UEFA Champions League football and came closer than ever to winning the Premier League trophy.

We battled Leicester City for the title almost until the very end, before an uncharacteristic final day 5-1 defeat at Newcastle dropped us into third.

Still, it was a memorable season: we played some scintillating football and scored some memorable goals, including Dele Alli's goal of the season at Crystal Palace.

Harry Kane's Premier League Golden Boot confirmed his standing on the world stage and Toby Alderweireld was voted Spurs' Player of the Year.

AUGUST

League table (as it stood): 15th

Manchester United 1-0 Spurs; Spurs 2-2 Stoke; Leicester 1-1 Spurs; Spurs 0-0 Everton

It was a frustrating start to the season: an unfortunate Kyle Walker own goal meant we left Old Trafford without reward. Next, two Stoke City goals in the closing 12 minutes denied us our first win of the season. Eric Dier put Spurs ahead and Nacer Chadli added a second, but two late goals earned Stoke a point. Dele Alli's first goal for Spurs put us ahead at Leicester, but our delight was short-lived: Riyad Mahrez cut in from the right, hitting an unstoppable shot into the far corner, and Leicester hit back for a draw. A spirited performance against Everton didn't get the result it deserved as we were held to a goalless draw at White Hart Lane.

SEPTEMBER

League table: 5th

Sunderland 0-1 Spurs; Spurs 1-0 Crystal Palace; Spurs 4-1 Manchester City

A great month for Tottenham Hotspur started with a hard-fought 1-0 win over Sunderland. Ryan Mason completed a well-worked move to give us our first League win of the season. Heung-Min Son scored his first League goal as we beat Crystal Palace 1-0 at White Hart Lane. The month ended in memorable fashion with a stunning 4-1 win over Manchester City. Eric Dier levelled just before half time before City were stunned with a three-goal salvo in the second period. Toby Alderweireld headed home his first Spurs goal to give us a 50th-minute lead and Harry Kane scored 11 minutes later. Erik Lamela then capped a superb effort by tucking home our fourth on 79 minutes. City were left reeling and unable to respond. After a number of heavy defeats to the visitors in recent seasons, this was a particularly sweet victory!

OCTOBER

League table: 6th

Swansea 2-2 Spurs; Spurs 0-0 Liverpool;
Bournemouth 1-5 Spurs

It was the Christian Eriksen show at Swansea as two superb free-kicks earned us a point at the Liberty Stadium. Spurs couldn't break down a Liverpool side looking to impress new manager Jürgen Klopp in a goalless draw at White Hart Lane. A Harry Kane hat-trick plus goals from Mousa Dembélé and Erik Lamela saw us thrash Bournemouth 5-1 at the Vitality Stadium. After being frustrated over the past few weeks, Bournemouth were the unfortunate opponents against a Spurs side hungry for goals.

PREMIER LEAGUE REVIEW

NOVEMBER

League table: 5th

Spurs 3-1 Aston Villa; Arsenal 1-1 Spurs; Spurs 3-1 West Ham; Spurs 0-0 Chelsea

November began with a comfortable win over struggling Aston Villa. Mousa Dembélé, Dele Alli and Harry Kane were on target. Alli's form was one of many plus points at this stage of the season. Kane was on the scoresheet again in the north London derby. Spurs dominated at The Emirates but a late Kieran Gibbs goal left us frustrated, going home with just a point. If Spurs were guilty of not taking their chances at Arsenal, we made sure of the points with a devastating display against West Ham. Two from Harry Kane plus goals from Toby Alderweireld and Kyle Walker made it 12 Premier League matches without defeat.

DECEMBER

League table: 3rd

West Brom 1-1 Spurs; Spurs 1-2 Newcastle; Southampton 0-2 Spurs; Spurs 3-0 Norwich; Watford 1-2 Spurs

December saw us move into the top four but the month didn't start so well. Dele Alli's brilliant goal wasn't enough to earn all three points at West Brom. Eight days later, Newcastle were victorious at White Hart Lane for the third successive season. Harry Kane scored a superb individual goal on his 100th appearance for Spurs at Southampton and Dele Alli added a second shortly before half-time. It was the Harry Kane show once again on Boxing Day as we beat Norwich 3-0 at White Hart Lane, Tom Carroll completing the scoring with a fine individual goal. The year ended in style with a 2-1 win at Watford: Erik Lamela put us ahead, Watford levelled, then Heung-Min Son popped up with a clever goal to earn all three points. The celebrations between players and supporters after the game became an iconic picture, adopting the hashtag #togetherthfc.

JANUARY

League table: 4th

Everton 1-1 Spurs; Spurs 0-1 Leicester;
Spurs 4-1 Sunderland; Crystal Palace 1-3 Spurs

The Toby Alderweireld and Dele Alli combination were in lethal form against Everton: Toby's perfect long ball found Dele, who volleyed in style, and we left Goodison Park with a point. Leicester scored a late winner on a frustrating night at White Hart Lane, although we recovered to comfortably beat Sunderland. Sam Allardyce's side took a shock lead but goals from Christian Eriksen (2), Mousa Dembélé and Harry Kane sealed a comfortable win. If people weren't talking about Dele Alli before we travelled to Crystal Palace they certainly were at full-time! Dele's incredible goal was voted Goal of the Season by various broadcasters and, more importantly, it put Spurs 2-1 ahead after Harry Kane had levelled. Nacer Chadli sealed the win in stoppage time.

FEBRUARY

League table: 2nd

Norwich 0-3 Spurs; Spurs 1-0 Watford;
Manchester City 1-2 Spurs; Spurs 2-1 Swansea

February was a month to remember. It started with an impressive win at Norwich: Dele Alli found the net once again before two more goals from Harry Kane sealed a 3-0 win. Watford frustrated us until an unlikely source found the net - Kieran Trippier scoring to earn three more valuable points for Spurs. We confirmed our place in the most fascinating title race in years when we beat Manchester City 2-1 at the Etihad. A Harry Kane penalty put Spurs ahead but when Kelechi Iheanacho levelled for City, they looked destined to win the match. However, birthday boy Christian Eriksen had other ideas, and his clinical finish earned a memorable victory in Manchester. Three days after UEFA Europa League action, we faced a determined Swansea side. We trailed for the majority of the match before Nacer Chadli levelled and Danny Rose scored the winner on 77 minutes. We finished the month in second, and excitement continued to grow at White Hart Lane.

MARCH

League table: 2nd

West Ham 1-0 Spurs; Spurs 2-2 Arsenal; Aston Villa 0-2 Spurs; Spurs 3-0 Bournemouth

It was a tough start to the month as a rare off-day saw us leave Upton Park pointless. We then faced the biggest north London derby for many years as Spurs and Arsenal chased the Premier League title. An Aaron Ramsey goal gave Arsenal a first-half lead, but after Francis Coquelin was sent off, Spurs took advantage with goals from Toby Alderweireld and a stunning effort from Harry Kane. We were, however, left frustrated, as Alexis Sanchez rescued a point for Arsenal. Later in the month Kane and Dele Alli were on target again as we beat Aston Villa, and Spurs ended March with a good win over Bournemouth. Kane opened the scoring after just 43 seconds, shortly after adding a second, while Christian Eriksen scored the third and final goal in the second half. Spurs finished the month in second, five points behind surprise leaders Leicester.

APRIL

League table: 2nd

Liverpool 1-1 Spurs; Spurs 3-0 Manchester Utd; Stoke 0-4 Spurs; Spurs 1-1 West Brom

By April, the Premier League title was looking like a two-horse race between Spurs and Leicester. In a difficult month we earned a point at Liverpool, thanks to a superb effort from Harry Kane, while eight days later three goals in six minutes saw us enjoy a fantastic win over Manchester United: Dele Alli, Toby Alderweireld and the ever-improving Erik Lamela with the goals. It would have been difficult to better that performance but Spurs continued to impress. Our next victims were Stoke City: Kane opened the scoring with a superb curling effort from outside the area while two from Dele Alli and another from Kane completed the rout. Our hopes of a first title since 1961 suffered a huge blow at the hands of West Brom: a Craig Dawson own goal gave Spurs a first-half lead, but he later made amends to equalise, handing Leicester a huge advantage at the top.

MAY

Final Position: 3rd

Chelsea 2-2 Spurs; Spurs 1-2 Southampton; Newcastle 5-1 Spurs

Leicester were confirmed champions after Spurs were held by Chelsea at Stamford Bridge. It looked to be going our way after Harry Kane and Heung-Min Son put us 2-0 ahead, but second-half goals from Gary Cahill and Eden Hazard rescued a point for a pumped-up Chelsea side determined to stop the title going to White Hart Lane. Son was on target again in our final home game but Southampton, still chasing European football, were victorious. The season ended in disappointment as we were beaten 5-1 at Newcastle, however we accomplished our highest-ever third place finish in the Premier League. Now, we have Champions League football to look forward to, with a young and exciting squad under Manager Mauricio Pochettino.

1	Leicester City	38	23	12	3	68	36	32	81
2	Arsenal	38	20	11	7	65	36	29	71
3	Tottenham Hotspur	38	19	13	6	69	35	34	70
4	Man. City	38	19	9	10	71	41	30	66
5	Man. United	38	19	9	10	49	35	14	66
6	Southampton	38	18	9	11	59	41	18	63
7	West Ham	38	16	14	8	65	51	14	62
8	Liverpool	38	16	12	10	63	50	13	60
9	Stoke City	38	14	9	15	41	55	-14	51
10	Chelsea	38	12	14	12	59	53	6	50
11	Everton	38	11	14	13	59	55	4	47
12	Swansea City	38	12	11	15	42	52	-10	47
13	Watford	38	12	9	17	40	50	-10	45
14	West Brom	38	10	13	15	34	48	-14	43
15	Crystal Palace	38	11	9	18	39	51	-12	42
16	Bournemouth	38	11	9	18	45	67	-22	42
17	Sunderland	38	9	12	17	48	62	-14	39
R	Newcastle	38	9	10	19	44	65	-21	37
R	Norwich City	38	9	7	22	39	67	-28	34
R	Aston Villa	38	3	8	27	27	76	-49	17

2015/2016 SEASON STATS

SUPPLIED BY OPTA

Games Played	38	

Attacking

		Rank
Goals	69	2
Ave Goals per game	1.82	2
Total Shots (excl blocked shots)	479	1
Shots on Target	252	1
% Shots on Target	52.6%	1
% Goals to Shots	14.4%	12
Touches in Opposition Box	883	7
Shots on Target Inside Box	168	2
Shots on Target Outside Box	84	1
% of Shots On Target from Inside Box	66.7%	-

Passing

Total Passes (Excl. Crosses & Corners)	18,649	6
Total Completed Passes (Excl. Crosses & Corners)	15,009	6
Overall Pass Completion %	80.5%	7
% Passes Long	13.7%	14
% Passes in Opposition Half	58.1%	15
% of Passes in Attacking Third	30.2%	15
Total Crosses & Corners	738	15
Cross Completion %	20.6%	16

Defending

Goals Conceded	35	1
Ave Goals conceded per game	0.92	1
Tackles	805	3
Interceptions	645	11
Blocks	138	8
Clearances	1046	5
Shots on Target Faced	122	20
Shots on Target Faced Inside Box	81	20

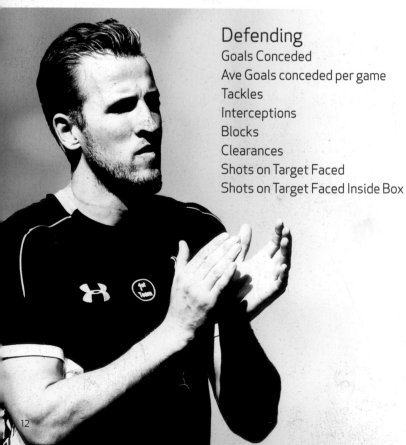

CAPITAL ONE CUP REVIEW

TOTTENHAM HOTSPUR 1 - 2 ARSENAL

Our League Cup campaign ended in the third round at White Hart Lane as Arsenal edged a competitive and entertaining derby.

The visitors took a half time lead after Mathieu Flamini tucked home in the 26th minute, but we were level again through a Calum Chambers own goal 12 minutes into the second period and were unfortunate not to take the lead during a spell of great pressure. But the Gunners secured a place in the fourth round when Flamini thumped in a 20-yard volley in the 78th minute and we were unable to peg them back again despite a late flurry of chances.

Both teams fielded much-changed sides in a busy period of the season.

GROUP J

TOTTENHAM HOTSPUR 3-1 QARABAĞ

Our Europa League Group J campaign started with a win over Qarabağ of Azerbaijan. Qarabağ took an early lead through a Richard Almeida penalty but Heung-Min Son scored a quick-fire double on his home debut and Erik Lamela added a third on 86 minutes.

MONACO 1-1 TOTTENHAM HOTSPUR

We looked set to make it two wins from two in Group J as we led through Erik Lamela's first-half goal and looked capable of adding a second after the break at Stade Louis II. However, Monaco levelled when two substitutes combined in the 81st minute, Nabil Dirar crossing for Stephan El Shaarawy to head home from close range.

ANDERLECHT 2-1 TOTTENHAM HOTSPUR

We paid the price for missed chances as Anderlecht consigned us to our first defeat in the group. Christian Eriksen opened the scoring on four minutes but Anderlecht levelled nine minutes later and won it late in the second half.

TOTTENHAM HOTSPUR 2-1 ANDERLECHT

Mousa Dembélé hit a stunning winner with just three minutes remaining to edge us past Anderlecht and send us to the top of Group J. Harry Kane had earlier given us a first-half lead before Anderlecht levelled.

QARABAĞ 0-1 TOTTENHAM HOTSPUR

Harry Kane scored in his sixth successive game to fire us into the knockout stages of the Europa League with a hard-fought win against Qarabağ in Baku.

TOTTENHAM HOTSPUR 4-1 MONACO

Top spot in Europa League Group J was safely secured at White Hart Lane thanks to a brilliant first half Erik Lamela hat-trick and Tom Carroll's first goal for Spurs.

EUROPA LEAGUE ROUND OF 32 - FIRST LEG

FIORENTINA 1-1 TOTTENHAM HOTSPUR

For the second successive season, we faced Fiorentina in the round of 32. Nacer Chadli opened the scoring from the penalty spot on 37 minutes. Fiorentina came back in the second-half and levelled as fortune went against us and Federico Bernardeschi's 30-yard shot deflected off Ryan Mason before looping home.

EUROPA LEAGUE ROUND OF 32 - SECOND LEG

TOTTENHAM HOTSPUR 3-0 FIORENTINA *(Spurs won 4-1 on aggregate)*

A comprehensive victory in the second leg saw us ease into the last 16. Ryan Mason set the ball rolling with a first-half opener, before Erik Lamela doubled our advantage. Fiorentina's captain Gonzalo Rodriguez then put through his own net to make it 3-0 on the night and 4-1 on aggregate.

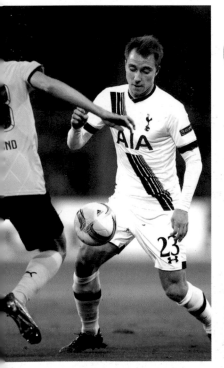

EUROPA LEAGUE ROUND OF 16 - FIRST LEG

BORUSSIA DORTMUND 3-0 TOTTENHAM HOTSPUR

Borussia Dortmund grabbed the upper hand in emphatic fashion by inflicting a heavy defeat in the first leg in Germany. With the Premier League now a priority, Mauricio Pochettino decided to make changes to his side and our starting 11 were well beaten with goals from the excellent Pierre-Emerick Aubameyang and a brace from Marco Reus.

EUROPA LEAGUE ROUND OF 16 - SECOND LEG

TOTTENHAM HOTSPUR 1-2 BORUSSIA DORTMUND *(Dortmund won 5-1 on aggregate)*

Our Europa League campaign came to an end at White Hart Lane as we suffered a 2-1 defeat to Borussia Dortmund and were beaten 5-1 on aggregate. It was always going to be a tough task to turn the tie around and it was made all the more difficult when Pierre-Emerick Aubameyang scored either side of half time to put Dortmund in the driving seat. We did find the target with 17 minutes remaining through Heung-Min Son – his sixth goal in eight games against Dortmund – but in the end for Spurs it was too little, too late.

THE EMIRATES FA CUP REVIEW

FA CUP 3RD ROUND

TOTTENHAM HOTSPUR 2-2 LEICESTER CITY

Harry Kane's first FA Cup goal for Spurs – his 50th for the Club – earned us a replay against Leicester City following late drama at White Hart Lane.

The Foxes led 2-1 with minutes to play and looked set to knock us out of the competition for the second successive season. However, redemption came in the form of an 89th minute penalty which Kane, who only came off the bench 20 minutes earlier, confidently tucked away.

It was no more than we deserved after dominating for long spells of the game, taking the lead through Christian Eriksen, before Marcin Wasilewski and Shinji Okazaki scored for Leicester either side of half-time.

FA CUP 3RD ROUND REPLAY

LEICESTER CITY 0-2 TOTTENHAM HOTSPUR

A brilliant effort from Heung-Min Son and a second through Nacer Chadli saw us get the better of Leicester City in the third round replay at the King Power Stadium.

After a relatively quiet opening spell, the game exploded into life six minutes before half-time when Son smashed home from the edge of the box. Chadli's cool finish settled the tie in the second half and secured a fourth round trip to Colchester United.

FA CUP 4TH ROUND

COLCHESTER UNITED 1-4 TOTTENHAM HOTSPUR

Nacer Chadli struck twice as Spurs eased into the fifth round of the FA Cup at Colchester United. Our first competitive visit to the Weston Homes Community Stadium saw a professional display for the TV cameras with Eric Dier and Tom Carroll also finding the net. Chadli opened the scoring; Dier added a second; Chadli netted the third and just two minutes after Ben Davies inadvertently turned into his own net, Carroll converted Chadli's cross from close range to earn a 4-1 win.

FA CUP 5TH ROUND

TOTTENHAM HOTSPUR 0-1 CRYSTAL PALACE

Our FA Cup hopes ended at White Hart Lane as Crystal Palace – who would go on to reach the final – knocked us out in the fifth round. Defender Martin Kelly scored the only goal of the game in first-half stoppage time following an entertaining 45 minutes which threw up chances for both sides. Spurs worked hard after the break to find an equaliser, but, despite our valiant efforts, it just wasn't to be.

HARRY KANE - "HE'S ONE OF OUR OWN!"

The name Harry Kane is now placed alongside the very best strikers in world football. The fears of a 'one season wonder' from those outside N17 after a stunning 2014/2015 campaign were shattered after another season to remember in 2015/2016.

After just one goal in his first nine in the Premier League, Harry responded superbly to post the highest goals total for a Spurs player in the Premier League with 25 goals, earning him the Premier League Golden Boot award. It was the first time a Spurs striker received the award since Teddy Sheringham's 22 goals in season 1992/1993. In fact, his 25 represented the highest league total since Gary Lineker's 28 in 1991/1992 and he became the first Spur since Martin Chivers (1970-1972) to score 20 goals back-to-back in a league campaign.

Harry said: "For me, it's about progressing, getting better as a player and as a person as well. A lot has changed in the last couple of years and it's all about how you take that on and respond to it. That makes you as a person. It's exciting times and hopefully I can keep on improving and with the squad here, the manager and the way the Club is moving forward I can only see us all getting better."

Harry is now a regular fixture in the England squad and started three out of the four matches at Euro 2016. It was a disappointing campaign for Harry and the squad but he insists the experience will be vital and, eventually, his Club will see the benefit of a striker determined to be the star name for Club and country. At just 22 at the time of the European Championships in France, the popular striker will have many more opportunities to impress for his country. After a well-earned break, Kane was quick to focus on the Club he loves and an exciting future at White Hart Lane and Wembley.

"We all feel we have a great thing going here, all moving in the right direction with a young and hungry squad. We want to keep improving, keep getting better and now we've had the taste of a Premier League title race we want to do it all over again."

Chelsea's point against us at Stamford Bridge last May meant Leicester City were crowned Premier League champions after an exciting race against Claudio Ranieri's side. It was a night Harry will never forget.

THE GOAL-DEN BOYS

Spurs players to finish top goalscorer in the top flight

1957/1958 - Bobby Smith 36 goals in Division One

1962/1963 - Jimmy Greaves 37 goals in Division One

1963/1964 - Jimmy Greaves 35 goals in Division One

1964/1965 - Jimmy Greaves 29 goals in Division One (tied with Andy McEvoy, Blackburn)

1968/1969 - Jimmy Greaves 27 goals in Division One

1980/1981 - Steve Archibald 20 goals in Division One (tied with Peter Withe, Villa)

1986/1987 - Clive Allen 33 goals in Division One (record 49 for a Spurs season, also won European Golden Boot as the top league goalscorer across all European leagues)

1989/1990 - Gary Lineker 24 goals in Division One

1992/1993 - Teddy Sheringham 22 goals (21 for us, one for Forest) in Premier League – introduction of PL Golden Boot, first winner

2015/2016 - Harry Kane 25 goals in Premier League (highest total for a Spurs player in a PL season).

"Seeing them acting like they had won the league and us disappointed, showed how far we have come and what type of team we have", he said. "We have to use everything that happened last season - good and bad - to our advantage. We have to take it all in, remember what it was like and use it for the seasons ahead."

It seems a lifetime ago when Harry was impressing in the Academy, culminating in loan moves to Leyton Orient, Millwall, Norwich and Leicester. Born in Walthamstow, Harry scored five goals in 18 games for Orient.

The following season, 2011/2012, saw his initial emergence at Spurs with a debut against Hearts and six appearances in the Europa League, including his first goal in a 4-0 victory at Shamrock Rovers. He finished the season with a successful loan spell at Millwall. He made his Premier League debut for Spurs at Newcastle on the opening day of the 2012/2013 season before a move to Norwich on loan, but a serious ankle injury restricted his appearances at Carrow Road. On his return to fitness, Harry joined Leicester City and helped them reach the Championship play-offs. It was in the latter part of the 2013/2014 season where Harry started to make an influence in the Spurs squad, featuring on 19 occasions, scoring four goals including his first Premier League goal in a 5-1 win over Sunderland. 2014/2015 was the campaign where he shot to fame. A stoppage time free-kick at Aston Villa in November was the start of his onslaught on Premier League defences after impressing in the Europa League. He went on to score 31 goals in 51 appearances in all competitions becoming the first Spurs player to break the 30-goal mark since Gary Lineker in 1991/1992. It was also the season that saw him earn a first cap and first England call and the PFA Young Player of the Year award.

Fast forward back to now, the boy from Walthamstow is one of the most dangerous strikers in world football and it goes without saying that he will be at the centre of any future success we enjoy.

SPOTLIGHT: TOBY ALDERWEIRELD

When you finish 3rd in the Premier League, it's a team effort. Certain players will receive individual awards. Harry Kane – Premier League Golden Boot. Dele Alli – Goal of the Season, but it was Toby Alderweireld who received your votes to secure the One Hotspur Members and Supporters' Clubs' Player of the Season.

Given so many impressed last season it only adds weight to just how remarkable Toby's season was at White Hart Lane. It wasn't just the Spurs fans who voted for Toby. He was selected in the PFA Team of the Season and UEFA Europa League Squad of the Season. It capped off a great first season for Toby and he says awards received from inside the Club mean a lot to him.

"It's a wonderful feeling. It's always nice to have something like this, especially for a defender as it's more difficult to win! I was honoured but it should or could have been another 15 players who deserved it as well but I was very happy with it and very proud. A lot of players deserved this award. It's difficult to describe - there are no words for it."

Toby joined Spurs from Atletico Madrid in July 2015 after a successful loan spell at Southampton. His performances in the Premier League alerted a number of clubs, but Alderweireld decided his future was best served at White Hart Lane. The Belgium international came through the ranks at Ajax, making 186 appearances and scoring 15 goals during nine years with the Eredivisie champions, where he lifted three league titles and one Dutch Cup.

Our title run last season only ended in May after a number of breath-taking displays throughout the season, but we had the defence to thank just as much as our attack. Spurs conceded 53 goals in Mauricio's first season in charge and an improved defence was top of his agenda in the summer of 2015. It's fair to say our Manager clearly identified the problem as we conceded just 35 goals last season and, of course, Toby played a vital role in that improvement. Toby's partnership with Jan Vertonghen for club and country helped earn Spurs consistent results, making them very hard to beat. Toby also formed a strong partnership with Kevin Wimmer after Jan suffered an injury midway through the season. A player in Toby's position can often be overlooked for the big prizes but he, more than any, makes a great case for the defence.

TOBY STATS

★ 35 goals conceded is our best in the Premier League and second-best of all-time in a top-flight season - bettered only by 33 in Division One in 1970/1971.

★ Best goal difference in the Premier League in 2015/2016, plus-34.

★ Joint-best record in terms of goals conceded in the Premier League for the season with Manchester United, who also conceded 35.

★ Toby was ever-present in the Premier League and Europa League, starting 49 of our 53 matches.

"He's been great for us and he's a great guy for the group as well, so relaxed and down to earth."
Jan Vertonghen on Toby

It's fair to say Dele's Spurs career couldn't have gone any better so far. The 2016 PFA Young Player of the Year continues to make headlines for his fantastic displays following his move from MK Dons.

Let's go back to August 2015. Dele stood out against Real Madrid in the Audi Cup, including a nutmeg on our former playmaker Luka Modric. His performance in Munich earned him a place on the bench at Manchester United on the opening day. His first Spurs goal soon followed at Leicester and earned him his first start at Sunderland the following month. He didn't look back after that becoming a regular starter. After nine competitive starts for his Club, England came calling, scoring a brilliant opener against France at Wembley. Goals against Southampton, Everton and Norwich followed but one in particular will stand out for the rest of his career. His effort at Crystal Palace won our own and the BBC Goal of the Season awards. Dele flicked the ball up over his head 20 yards from goal before turning and volleying low inside the near post in the 84th minute. "It was a bit of a natural thing. I didn't really think about it too much and I sort of shocked myself – I think you could tell from my celebration, I didn't really know what to do."

To finish his first season in the Premier League with 10 goals was hugely impressive and it all ended with Dele being named PFA Young Player of the Year and earning a place in the PFA Premier League Team of the Year along with Club team-mates Harry Kane, Toby Alderweireld and Danny Rose.

A fantastic, humble character around the training centre, Dele's friendship with Eric Dier is well documented. Their impressive partnership on the pitch was a key factor in our success last season. Supporters enjoyed following their friendship off the pitch, too as both used social media to give the fans access to their routine when they were away from Hotspur Way. "He was one of the first who made me feel welcome like a big brother. He had only been at the Club for a year. We have a lot of banter with each other. He tries to wind me up but I know I wind him up!"

DELE ON THE NOW FAMOUS WAVE:

"I didn't realise it was going to be as famous as what it is. I first did it before we played Manchester United at MK Dons. Then, when I joined Spurs, someone found it on the internet and it went on from there."

PFA YOUNG PLAYER OF THE YEAR

1979/1980 - Glenn Hoddle
2011/2012 - Kyle Walker
2012/2013 - Gareth Bale
2014/2015 - Harry Kane
2015/2016 - Dele Alli

"HE'S MAGIC, YOU KNOW"

Now in his third season at the Club, Mauricio can comfortably say the current squad is the one he built. The Argentinian signed an extension to his contract in May 2016, much to the delight of all Spurs supporters. In his first season in charge, he guided us to a fifth place finish in the Premier League and a League Cup final. One of the many reasons for his appointment was his reputation for developing young players into the First team. He has continued in that vein at White Hart Lane, assembling a squad with the youngest average age in the Premier League in season 2015/2016, securing a place in the top three.

The season ended in disappointment after an unlikely push for a first title since 1961, but after time to reflect, a top three finish certainly exceeded expectations in only his second season, finishing above the likes of Manchester City, Manchester United, Chelsea and Liverpool. As we enter a new year, Mauricio said: "Now is an exciting period for Tottenham Hotspur with the facilities we have, the new stadium, we have unbelievable staff and players. We have an exciting period ahead and I'm happy to be here to try and help the Club to be successful in the next few years."

Mauricio is determined to be successful in a special period in this great Club's history.. "It's true that our ambition is to win trophies," he said. "To achieve Champions League football is fantastic and we need to keep that level and try to look ahead and try to challenge for trophies. We need to push ourselves to try to improve individually and collectively."

Managers are often criticised for not showing emotion and not being in touch with supporters, but Mauricio is quite the opposite. His embrace for every player after our brilliant 2-1 win at Manchester City last season was a moment to remember. In fact, it became a common theme at away grounds, Mauricio applauding and bowing to our magnificent away support and in return they sang the catchy song: "He's magic, you knowwwww, Mauricio Pochettino" to the tune of the 1970s classic 'Magic' by Pilot. Simple, but effective and clever with a difficult surname to work on. The fans love him, he loves them, a relationship we hope that will last for a very long time.

> "WE (THE COACHES) CAN FEEL THE APPRECIATION OF EVERYONE HERE – THERE IS NO BETTER PLACE TO BE RIGHT NOW."

MEET MAURICIO'S TEAM:

Jesús Pérez – Assistant Manager
Jesús followed 'Poch' to Spurs in May 2014 after a successful spell as Southampton Assistant Manager. Jesús also worked alongside him at Espanyol as Fitness Coach. Born in Spain, Jesús has coached for 18 years at Al Ittihad, Almeria, Rayo Vallecano, Pontevedra, Real Murcia, Castellon and Tarragona.

Miguel D'Agostino – First Team Coach
Miguel, like Jesús, followed Mauricio Pochettino to White Hart Lane from Southampton. He played alongside Pochettino for Argentinian side Newell's Old Boys in the early 1990s. After leaving French side Brest as Chief Scout, he joined Pochettino's coaching staff at Espanyol.

Toni Jiménez – Goalkeeping Coach
After leaving Barcelona, Toni had a brief spell at Rayo Vallecano, before making over 200 appearances for Espanyol, where he met then team-mate Mauricio Pochettino. Toni won three caps for Spain and won a gold medal for Spain in the 1992 Olympics. He returned to Espanyol as Assistant Coach to Mauricio, before following him to Southampton.

AVERAGE AGE OF PREMIER LEAGUE STARTING 11s IN 2015/2016

Team	Average age	Team	Average age
Spurs	24 years, 328 days	Sunderland	27 years, 276 days
Liverpool	25 years, 241 days	Stoke	27 years, 290 days
Newcastle	25 years, 337 days	AFC Bournemouth	28 years, 12 days
Man Utd	26 years, 8 days	Swansea	28 years, 42 days
Everton	26 years, 306 days	Leicester	28 years, 51 days
Southampton	26 years, 322 days	Crystal Palace	28 years, 55 days
West Ham	26 years, 348 days	Norwich	28 years, 62 days
Aston Villa	27 years, 35 days	Man City	28 years, 253 days
Chelsea	27 years, 112 days	Watford	28 years, 257 days
Arsenal	27 years, 142 days	West Brom	29 years, 197 days

PLAYER PROFILES

HUGO LLORIS

Our Club captain is now in his fifth season at the Club. Hugo featured on 46 occasions last season after quickly recovering from a wrist injury in the summer of 2015. Regarded as one of the best goalkeepers in the world.

MICHEL VORM

Dutch international goalkeeper joined us from Swansea in the summer of 2014. Michel made seven appearances last season for Spurs including our first match of 2015/2016 against Manchester United.

KIERAN TRIPPIER

Kieran joined Spurs from Burnley in June 2015 and competed with Kyle Walker for our right-back spot last season, featuring on 19 occasions in all competitions. He scored the winner against Watford in our 1-0 home win in February 2016.

KYLE WALKER

One of our longest-serving players, Kyle enjoyed a fine 2015/2016 campaign in which he started 33 of our 38 Premier League games and scored a memorable goal in a 4-1 home victory over West Ham. He was also England's first choice right-back during Euro 2016.

JAN VERTONGHEN

Now in his fifth season at the Club, Jan formed an impressive partnership with Toby Alderweireld last season. The duo remained ever-present in the Premier League until Jan picked up a knee ligament injury in January 2016, but the Belgian returned to the side in the closing weeks of the campaign and made 33 season appearances in total.

25

TOBY ALDERWEIRELD

Our Player of the Year in just his first season at the Club, Toby also earned a place in the PFA Team of the Season. Toby played every minute of every game in the Europa League and Premier League, barring a couple of minutes at the end of our 2-2 draw with Chelsea in May as he was forced off in stoppage time.

He also weighed in with four goals – all at home in the Premier League – against Manchester City, West Ham, Arsenal and Manchester United.

KEVIN WIMMER

Central defender Kevin joined us from Cologne in May 2015 and proved to be superb cover for the injured Jan Vertonghen. Kevin made his debut against Crystal Palace in January 2016 and went on to make a total 21 appearances for the Club in his first full season. In July, Kevin's performances were rewarded with a new five-year contract committing his future to the Club.

BEN DAVIES

Exciting young Welsh left-back joined Spurs in July 2014. He made 27 appearances in all competitions during the 2015/2016 campaign, once again battling Danny Rose for position. Ben impressed for Wales at left-back during Euro 2016 and remains an important member of the squad for his Club.

DANNY ROSE

Danny enjoyed another tremendous campaign in 2015/2016 ending in a starting role for England at Euro 2016. Once again competing for his spot with Ben Davies, he made 30 appearances in all competitions, scoring once – the winning goal against Swansea City at White Hart Lane in February 2016 – and impressing enough to be included in the PFA Team of the Year along with team-mates Toby Alderweireld, Dele Alli and Harry Kane.

ERIC DIER

Now a key member in the starting 11 for club and country, Eric enjoyed a brilliant season in a holding midfield role resulting in an England call-up. He went on to score in England's opening Euro 2016 match against Russia with a stunning free-kick. Eric started all bar one of our Premier League games during the 2015/2016 season, only missing out on the Liverpool home game in October 2015 through suspension.

MOUSA DEMBÉLÉ

Mousa enjoyed a brilliant 2015/2016 campaign resulting in a new long-term contract. He was a crucial member of the Spurs side that finished third and made 35 appearances in all competitions during that campaign. He also enjoyed a run of scoring in three consecutive games between October and November – a trio of goals that ended with a stunner against Anderlecht in the Europa League – and ended the term with four goals under his belt.

GEORGES-KEVIN NKOUDOU

The French Under-21 international joined Spurs on deadline day. Known for his speed, he made 41 appearances in all competitions for Marseille last season, scoring 10 times and producing five assists. He was particularly prolific in the Europa League where four of his goals came.

DELE ALLI

Since his move from MK Dons in 2015 Dele has enjoyed a rapid rise, culminating in a place in the England team for Euro 2016. He scored one of the goals of the season with a tremendous flick, turn and volley in a 3-1 victory at Crystal Palace in January 2016, and finished the campaign with a total of 10 Premier League goals and 46 appearances in all competitions. He was also named PFA Young Player of the Year and earned a spot in the PFA Premier League Team of the Year.

TOM CARROLL

After a successful loan spell at Swansea, Tom made 30 appearances for us in all competitions during 2015/2016, 12 of which were starts, and scored his first three senior goals for us against Monaco in the Europa League, Norwich City in the Premier League and Colchester United in the FA Cup.

ERIK LAMELA

Erik enjoyed a tremendous 2015/2016 campaign, establishing himself in our regular starting 11 with a string of committed displays. Erik scored 11 goals during the season – five in the Premier League and six in the Europa League – including his first hat-trick in a 4-1 home win over Monaco in December 2015. He finished the season having made 44 appearances in all competitions.

JOSHUA ONOMAH

Josh is now a member of the first team after a breakthrough season in the 2015/2016 campaign. Having initially made his senior debut in an FA Cup third round replay victory against Burnley in January 2015, he made 19 First Team appearances in all competitions during last season, including a Premier League bow against Aston Villa in November 2015, and a first start against Monaco in the Europa League a month later.

CHRISTIAN ERIKSEN

The Danish international enjoyed another memorable campaign in 2015/2016. Christian made 47 appearances in all competitions and scored eight goals, including a coolly-taken late winner away at Manchester City on his birthday in February 2016.

VICTOR WANYAMA

Victor joined us from Southampton in June 2016. The tough-tackling midfielder worked under Manager Mauricio Pochettino at St Mary's. Wanyama made his international debut for Kenya at just 15 years of age and now captains his country.

HEUNG-MIN SON

'Sonny' joined us from Bayer Leverkusen in August 2015. The South Korean international scored twice on his home debut in a 3-1 Europa League victory over Qarabağ before netting the only goal of the game against Crystal Palace three days later. A foot injury side-lined him for a spell and he finished the 2015/2016 campaign having scored eight goals in 40 appearances, with one of his highlights proving to be his last-gasp winner at Watford in December 2015.

VINCENT JANSSEN

Vincent joined Spurs in July 2016. The Dutch international scored an incredible 27 league goals for AZ Alkmaar before moving to White Hart Lane. Janssen scored three goals in five games for Holland including a goal against England at Wembley prior to his move to N17. His performances also earned him the 2016 Johan Cruyff Trophy, awarded to the Eredivisie's Young Player of the Year, which has previously been won by Rafael van der Vaart and Christian Eriksen.

HARRY KANE

Harry claimed the Premier League's Golden Boot with a 25-goal haul in 2015/2016. He scored 28 goals in 50 appearances in all competitions and became only the second Spurs player behind Teddy Sheringham in 1992/1993 to win the Premier League's Golden Boot and set a new Club record for goals in a Premier League season. He was named Premier League Player of the Month for March 2016, and earned a spot in the PFA Premier League Team of the Year. He finished the season as the lone striker for England in the opening two games in Euro 2016.

MOUSSA SISSOKO

Moussa joined Spurs on transfer deadline day from Newcastle. The France international impressed during Euro 2016, featuring for his country at every level from Under-16. Moussa represented Newcastle on 133 occasions, scoring 12 times.

2016/2017

WHITE HOT MOMENTS

White Hart Lane is one of the most iconic stadiums in football and supporters have witnessed many memorable matches. Regardless of your age, you'll have a favourite moment, and we've selected three matches for every generation to enjoy!

Spurs 10-4 Everton – 11 October 1958

The incredible score line might stand out, but this game was special for one reason – Bill Nicholson's first match in charge of Spurs. Bill, of course, led the Club to greater heights than we had ever reached. The players were only aware of his appointment just before kick-off, but goalscorer Terry Medwin insisted the squad already respected him as a player and would now do so as their manager. Alfie Stokes fired home after two minutes, but Everton soon levelled through Jimmy Harris. Next came an 'avalanche' of goals as a brace from Bobby Smith, plus goals from Stokes, Medwin and George Robb saw us surge into a 6-1 lead before the first half was out.

Everton, despite being humbled by the scoreline, had not looked a bad side, and after the interval, Harris completed his hat-trick, while Bobby Collins was responsible for the visitors' fourth goal.
Nicholson's new charges, though, were rampant, and two further goals from Smith, one from Tommy Harmer and a late strike from John Ryden completed a stunning scoreline.

It was the beginning of the most successful period in the Club's history and Bill remains our greatest manager of all time.

Spurs 1-1 Anderlecht – UEFA Cup Final 2nd leg – 23 May 1984

Not many clubs can say they have won a major trophy in their own stadium, but in May 1984, Spurs fans witnessed one of the most memorable nights at White Hart Lane. The Belgian side arrived in N17 level at 1-1 after the first leg. The second leg saw a 46,000 crowd and millions watching at home on TV. It nearly

ended in heartbreak as Anderlecht were ahead 2-1 on aggregate with under 10 minutes remaining, but Micky Hazard found Graham Roberts to equalise to send the game into extra time. We then won a dramatic penalty shoot-out as Tony Parks earned hero status with two penalty saves. The fans played their part in one of the Club's greatest 'glory, glory nights' and they certainly haven't been forgotten by the men who lifted the trophy. Winger Tony Galvin said: "It's my favourite memory without a doubt, mainly because we actually won it here in front of our own fans. To see the crowd so happy, pleased, ecstatic at the end of the game was a wonderful feeling and never bettered when I was playing football."

Spurs 3-1 Inter Milan – 2 November 2010

One for the younger generation. Our first appearance in the group stage format of the Champions League was one to remember. Not many gave us a chance to qualify from a group consisting of Champions League holders Inter Milan, German champions Werder Bremen and Dutch Champions FC Twente, but victory at home to Inter put us top of the group with two matches remaining. The atmosphere was electric and rekindles memories of the famous 'glory, glory nights'. It was also the night Gareth Bale firmly introduced himself onto the world stage. After scoring a brilliant hat-trick in the San Siro in the reverse fixture, it seemed impossible he could replicate that form for this match, but, despite not ending up on the scoresheet, he produced a masterclass to help Spurs beat the Italian side. Bale gave Inter's Maicon a torrid time down the left wing with his pace and power and crossed perfectly for Peter Crouch and Roman Pavlyuchenko to score. A stunning result at White Hart Lane.

Victor became our first signing of the summer, joining from Southampton.

The Kenya international didn't need an extra second to decide his future was destined for White Hart Lane. Victor's a proud Kenyan, and back home, they celebrated his move to N17, even the President of Kenya congratulated him via Twitter! He's the first Kenyan to score in the Champions League during his stint at Celtic after netting against Barcelona at Parkhead. He was also the first man from his country to grace the Premier League when Mauricio took him to Southampton in July 2013.

The 25-year-old was born in Nairobi. He left Kenya in 2007 to join Swedish side Helsingborg. A move to Belgian side Beerschot AC followed and impressive performances there earned him a move to Celtic in July 2011. Wanyama immediately became a key member of the side, helping them to the Premiership and Scottish Cup double in 2012/2013. His performances earned him the Scottish Premiership's Young Player of the Year award. He joined Southampton in the summer of 2013 and immediately impressed supporters, helping them finish 8th, 7th and 6th in his three seasons at the club. During that time he made 97 appearances in all competitions, scoring four goals.

At international level, Victor made his debut for Kenya at just 15 years of age and has since gone on to become captain of the national side. Despite the huge change in his life, Victor insists he'll never forget how it all began. "I started in the streets. I used to go to play football with my friends and sometimes we'd walk something like 10 kilometres just to go and play with some other guys. That's how I started getting interested in football. Also I enjoyed watching and following the Premier League. That's how my journey started.
We used to play in the street with bare feet. The pitches weren't so good but it was also a good experience and I believe that made me strong and helped in my upbringing. It was a hard way to grow as a player but it was really good."

With Mousa Dembélé, Eric Dier and now Victor, it's fair to say opposition sides are going to have a tough time getting past our midfield and Mauricio believed Victor had a number of qualities that he's already brought to the side. "I knew Victor very well because we signed him from Celtic to bring him to Southampton three years ago and I think he's a player that improves our squad and can help us for the next few years. He's a very strong midfielder who is a holding midfielder but can play free and can play very well with the ball. He's powerful and I think he's a perfect player for us."

The tenacious central midfielder made it clear Spurs was the Club for him with or without Champions League football but admits playing the very best in the world excites him as we look to progress through our group. "Here at Spurs, playing against top teams – it's only going to make us better and if you brush shoulders with the world's best players then nothing is impossible." Victor will also be part of a side making history – the last members of the Spurs squad to play at White Hart Lane, a stadium he always loved to visit as an opposing player. "It's great walking out of the tunnel and seeing the home fans cheering on the team. From outside you can see that the Club has a great fan base and that's one of the things that attracted me here."

```
V N D F D M N K X M L L
Q D R P Q E P W Z K L B
K J D M X A M C K O D R
Y E S O R M J B R V I X
W Y R C Y A L I E L E N
N J T K C Y S V L L R B
N B L Z N N Y A G V E N
Y F N F D A Z M L R Q Y
G C X T T W M T N L L V
A L D E R W E I R E L D
G T K M P X D L P Q R V
R W K A N E K L H R W C
```

Alderweireld
Alli
Dembélé
Dier
Kane
Lloris
Rose
Wanyama

SPOTLIGHT: VINCENT JANSSEN

"Never give up" - that's the message from Vincent Janssen. Our talented striker became the second signing of the summer after arriving from AZ Alkmaar. It's been a long road to success for the Netherlands international. For many, being released from a football club at 19 could signal the end for a player aspiring to play top level football, but not Vincent. After being released by Feyenoord he joined Almere City in the second tier of Dutch football. After scoring 32 goals in two seasons, he was back in the top division with AZ Alkmaar in 2015. His one season at AZ was truly phenomenal. He scored 27 goals, topping the Dutch goalscoring charts and he was awarded the Young Player of the Year award in Holland. It wasn't only at club level where he impressed, Vincent scored three goals in his first five matches for his country and is now a regular in a squad looking to qualify for the 2018 World Cup.

It's fair to say his record for AZ was somewhat unexpected. It certainly put him on the European map as a number of clubs began monitoring his situation. Vincent now reflects on a job well done after a tough start to his career.

"I had to go away from Feyenoord and I was thinking to myself 'I've got to work harder' because I wanted to go back to the Dutch Premier League, the Eredivisie. When I left Feyenoord the only thing I thought was that I would come back stronger. I was very happy that it happened because I did a lot for it. I know I can score goals as a striker but the second half of last season was incredible. We did such a nice job. At the end, we finished fourth so for the club that was very good."

Vincent is our seventh Dutch player to pull on our famous white shirt in league football. However, the first Dutch player on our books was Geert Van Driel in 1914. He spent five years at the Club featuring during the Football League's break for World War I. Johnny Metgod was our first Dutch player to feature in league football. He played 14 times for us in the 1987/1988 season after joining us from Forest. Second was Hans Segers, who made two appearances in 1998 and was part of our coaching staff until 2007. Willem Korsten joined us from Vitesse Arnhem in 1999 and made 27 appearances before injury forced him to retire in 2001. Edgar Davids was the first Dutch player to gain a cap on our books after coming off the bench against Macedonia in 2005. That was his 74th and last international cap. The midfielder joined us from Inter Milan in August 2005 and made 44 appearances before moving back to Ajax in January 2007.

Rafael van der Vaart joined us from Real Madrid on transfer deadline day in August 2010. A Real fans' favourite, Rafa scored 28 goals in 77 appearances before leaving for Hamburg in 2012. Vincent joins Michel Vorm in the squad. Michel joined us from Swansea in the summer of 2014.

Like Vorm, it didn't take long for Vincent to settle into the squad. Given his record in the Dutch league last season, it was little surprise a number of clubs were chasing his signature but he insists it was Spurs and only Spurs he wanted to play for.

"It's a beautiful Club, I can grow with this group, it's a very talented group and we're in the Champions League as well, so that's very nice. I hope to score a lot of goals and to win prizes."

SPURS AT WEMBLEY!

We hope you're enjoying your Wembley experience so far. Our move to the national stadium for Champions League matches was necessary in order to meet UEFA requirements, which will be impacted by the works in and around the current stadium affecting access, capacity and rights delivery.

As we will be required to vacate White Hart Lane to complete the latter stages of our new stadium and surrounding environs, the agreement additionally provides an option to play all of our Premier League and cup home games at Wembley Stadium for the 2017/2018 season. It is our intention to open the new stadium for the 2018/2019 season, with the timetable dependent on infrastructure, transport and associated commitments being delivered by TfL and Haringey Council.

Chairman Daniel Levy said: "Our season ticket waiting list is over 50,000 so this now also offers us a great opportunity to provide more of our supporters with a chance to see the team play live during our Champions League campaign."

INTERNATIONAL SPURS

International weekend on Hotspur Way can be a quiet time with many of the team away playing for their country. As you can see, Spurs have many international players, from all over the world.

KYLE WALKER, ENGLAND

HARRY KANE, ENGLAND

DANNY ROSE, ENGLAND

ERIC DIER, ENGLAND

DELE ALLI, ENGLAND

ERIK LAMELA, ARGENTINA

KEVIN WIMMER, AUSTRIA

JAN VERTONGHEN, BELGIUM

TOBY ALDERWEIRELD, BELGIUM

MOUSA DEMBÉLÉ, BELGIUM

CHRISTIAN ERIKSEN, DENMARK

HUGO LLORIS, FRANCE

VICTOR WANYAMA, KENYA

VINCENT JANSSEN, NETHERLANDS

HEUNG-MIN SON, SOUTH KOREA

BEN DAVIES, WALES

MOUSSA SISSOKO, FRANCE

SPURS LEGENDS

DO YOU WANT TO KNOW WHY TOTTENHAM HOTSPUR IS SUCH A SPECIAL CLUB? Regardless of league positions, Spurs have always attracted world-class talent. Some developed into White Hart Lane legends. In 2014 we remembered Jimmy Greaves, Jürgen Klinsmann, Dave Mackay, Ricky Villa and Pat Jennings. In 2015, it was Ossie Ardiles, Teddy Sheringham, Danny Blanchflower, Steve Perryman and Martin Chivers. In 2016, we introduced Gary Lineker, Alan Mullery, Ray Clemence, Paul Gascoigne and Chris Waddle. Below are five more greats who have graced the White Hart Lane turf.

GLENN HODDLE

Considered the most naturally gifted English player of his generation, Glenn Hoddle was a White Hart Lane hero for 12 years. He had sublime skills, unequalled passing ability and an eye for a goal as well as the knack of being able to turn a game around with a moment of magic.

Glenn was a key member of the Spurs team of the early 1980s who won two FA Cups and the UEFA Cup, although injury ruled him out of the European final. He also appeared in the 1987 FA Cup and 1982 League Cup Finals.

He featured in almost 500 competitive games before moving to Monaco in 1987. He returned to Spurs as manager in 2001 but his time as a player are our greatest memories of a man many called 'God' during his time at White Hart Lane. Glenn earned 53 England caps and would later manage his country for the 1998 World Cup campaign.

LEDLEY KING

One of our greatest ever captains. Ledley King made his debut against Liverpool in May 1999 and was a one-club man, which is rare in modern-day football. Ledley continued to impress at both centre-back and defensive midfield but would settle in one position and become one of the greatest defenders Spurs have ever had.

Ledley earned 21 caps for England but that would have been significantly more if he wasn't ravaged by injury during his career. His well-documented knee problem restricted him from training on a regular basis, meaning he would have to be carefully nurtured game-by-game. One of his greatest moments as captain was lifting the League Cup after beating Chelsea at Wembley in 2008. Once described by Thierry Henry as the best defender he had played against, he left managers amazed at his performances, despite so little training.

Ledley's testimonial night on 12 May 2014 was a night to remember and, as we said goodbye to his playing career, there wasn't a dry eye in the stadium. Ledley remains an important part of the Club, serving as a Club ambassador and has also helped coach our academy sides.

MARTIN PETERS

Martin joined us from West Ham in March 1970 for a British record fee of £200,000 and played a pivotal role in our trophy success in the early 1970s. He arrived as a World Cup winner, scoring in the final.

Martin made 260 appearances for us and scored 76 goals before departing for Norwich City in March 1975. He helped us lift the League Cup in 1971 and 1973 and the UEFA Cup, starting both finals at Wembley, plus Wolves and Feyenoord in 1972.

Martin was inducted into the Tottenham Hotspur Hall of Fame in March 2016 and still attends White Hart Lane on a regular basis.

CLIVE ALLEN

Clive Allen joined Spurs in 1984 and scored 84 goals in 135 appearances. In the 1986/1987 season he scored an incredible 49 goals – a record goals return in a single season. Clive joined Spurs after impressing at Queens Park Rangers and Crystal Palace, and after scoring twice against Everton on his debut at Goodison Park it was clear Spurs had signed a natural goal-scorer. Injury restricted him in his first season as Spurs finished third and it was a case of what might have been if he had been fit for the entire season. Clive returned to Spurs in a coaching capacity in 2007 and remains a frequent visitor to the Lane.

GARY MABBUTT

A model professional and fantastic captain, Gary played over 600 games for Spurs in 16 years before retiring at the end of the 1997/1998 Season.

Gary joined Spurs from Bristol Rovers for £105,000 in August 1982. Two years later, he helped us lift the UEFA Cup. His proudest moment in a Spurs shirt came in 1991, captaining the side that beat Nottingham Forest 2-1 at Wembley in a memorable game after beating Arsenal 3-1 in the famous semi-final. Gary earned 16 England caps and was awarded the MBE.

He is now a Club ambassador, travelling around the world representing our famous Club.

RISING STARS

AFTER IMPRESSING IN PRE-SEASON, FOUR YOUNGSTERS FROM OUR ACADEMY ARE NOW IN MAURICIO POCHETTINO'S THOUGHTS FOR 2017.

CAMERON CARTER-VICKERS

BORN: 31 December 1997
POSITION: Defender
JOINED SPURS: 01 July 2014

After featuring in all of our First Team pre-season friendlies, Cameron is now part of Mauricio Pochettino's squad. The strong centre-half regularly captained our Under-21 side last season and signed a new contract with the Club in October 2015. First Team football isn't totally new to Cameron after making it onto the bench on four occasions in the Europa League between December 2015, and March 2016.

In addition, Cameron played for the USA Under-20 national team at the FIFA Under-20 World Cup in New Zealand in the summer of 2015 and also played for the States at Under-17 and Under-23 levels while only 16.

SHAYON HARRISON

BORN: 13 July 1997
POSITION: Striker
JOINED SPURS: 01 July 2013

For Shayon Harrison, pre-season 2016/2017 will be one he'll never forget. After featuring on our tour of Australia, Shayon was included in the squad that beat Inter Milan 6-1, scoring our sixth goal of the game and his first at senior level. Shayon scored nine goals in 13 league appearances for our Under-21s last season, including a hat-trick in a 3-1 win over Sunderland at White Hart Lane in April 2016.

He also scored twice in three Premier League Under-21 International Cup appearances, signed a new contract with the Club in December 2015. His form at under-21 level earned him invaluable experience training with the First Team during our Europa League campaign.

MARCUS EDWARDS

BORN: 03 December 1998
POSITION: Attacking midfielder
JOINED SPURS: 01 July 2015

It's difficult not to get excited by Marcus Edwards. After a number of eye-catching performances for our Under-18 side, Marcus was selected to travel with the First Team for our tour of Australia. He immediately impressed after being introduced in the second half against Juventus. His performance in that game and then against Inter Milan have led to calls for him to feature in the First Team this season.

HARRY WINKS

BORN: 02 February 1996
POSITION: Midfielder
JOINED SPURS: 01 July 2012

Harry is one of our more experienced youngsters who continues to impress. The central midfielder was named on our First Team bench on a number of occasions last season. He made substitute appearances in the Europa League against Qarabağ and Fiorentina in addition to featuring 11 times for the Under-21s including two starts in the Premier League International Cup. He made his First Team debut when he went on as a substitute in a 1-0 Europa League group stage win over Partizan Belgrade in November 2014. Harry has also been capped by England at Under-17, Under-18, Under-19 and Under-20 levels.

SUPER SPURS QUIZ

It's a grand old team to play for and it's a grand old team to see, so if you know your history, try this 2017 Super Size Spurs Quiz.

1. Who did we face on the opening day this season?
2. Who scored our goal of the season in 2015/2016?
3. Victor Wanyama is from which nation?
4. Name our Champions League group opponents.
5. Our new stadium will have a capacity of 56,000 or 61,000?
6. How many goals did Harry Kane score in the Premier League last season?
7. Name our three squad members who featured for Belgium at Euro 2016.

8. Who scored against Russia in England's opening match of Euro 2016?

9. True or false – Spurs won the UEFA Cup (Europa League) in 1984
10. On how many occasions have Spurs won the League Cup?
11. Who do we face in our final match at White Hart Lane this season?
12. Who captained Spurs to the 1991 FA Cup?
13. Who scored our winning goal to secure a 2-1 win at Manchester City last season?

14. Kyle Walker arrived from which League One side in summer 2009?

TOTTENHAM HOTSPUR
is proud to present

PLAY GAMES

WIN MEDALS

Tottenham Turfies

It's a mini pitch invasion!

AT WHITE HART LANE THERE'S A WELL-KEPT SECRET... THERE'S SOMETHING IN THE TURF!

Tottenham Turfies are living in the pitch! They're our secret weapon that power up the players, fire up the fans, and create that Spurs magic at White Hart Lane

100% FREE

NOW YOU CAN JOIN IN WITH THE FUN TOO!

- Visit our online experience to create your own Turfie so you can be part of the Turfie gang!
- With your Turfie you can earn coins, win medals, collect player cards to share with friends, enter competitions, polls, quizzes and much, much more!

EARN COINS

START PLAYING TODAY AT

TottenhamTurfies.com

TURFIE CODE
ENTER THIS CODE FOR A BONUS REWARD!
ANNUAL

PRE-SEASON REPORT

With a number of First Team squad members unavailable after featuring at Euro 2016, Manager Mauricio Pochettino included a number of players from the Academy for our International Champions Cup campaign in Melbourne. The experience they gained playing two world class opponents was invaluable and some played their way into Pochettino's plans for the season ahead.

INTERNATIONAL CHAMPIONS CUP

Juventus 2-1 Tottenham Hotspur

An inexperienced Spurs side went close against Italian champions Juventus. Early goals from Paulo Dybala and Medhi Benatia put Juventus 2-0 ahead at half time. Erik Lamela was introduced as a second half substitute and ran the game, scoring and then denied by goalkeeper Neto late on as we chased an equaliser. New arrivals Victor Wanyama and Vincent Janssen both played their first games in our colours and played alongside Academy graduates including the impressive Harry Winks and Marcus Edwards.

Spurs:

Vorm; Trippier (Walkes 63), Ball (Amos 79), Carter-Vickers, Miller (Yedlin 46); Mason (c, Winks 46), Wanyama; Son (Lamela 46), Carroll (Edwards 63), Chadli (Onomah 46); Janssen (Harrison 63). Substitutes (not used): McGee, Glover, Walker-Peters.

INTERNATIONAL CHAMPIONS CUP

Atletico Madrid 1-0 Tottenham Hotspur

Goalkeeper Jan Oblak and the post denied Spurs in match where we deserved at least a draw against the Champions League finalists. Over 47,000 witnessed another impressive performance from the young Spurs side. Josh Onomah and Erik Lamela hit the frame of the goal, while Ryan Mason and Vincent Janssen were denied by two fine Oblak saves. Diego Godin scored for Atletico shortly before half time.

Spurs:
Vorm (McGee 75); Trippier (Walker-Peters 60), Walkes, Carter-Vickers, Yedlin (Miller 60); Wanyama (Mason 46), Winks (Ball 75); Lamela (Son 46), Eriksen (c, Carroll 46), Onomah (Chadli 60); Janssen (Edwards 75). Substitutes (not used): Glover, Amos, Harrison.

FRIENDLY

Inter Milan 1-6 Tottenham Hotspur

It was a full squad as our pre-season campaign ended in perfect fashion as we hit Inter Milan for six at the Ullevaal Stadion in Oslo. Many, including Harry Kane tasted their first match of the new season and he didn't look rusty scoring twice, first a penalty to put us ahead and his second was a fine right-footed drive. Erik Lamela put us 2-1 ahead with a superb effort from outside the area. Dele Alli put us 4-1 ahead after a clever assist from Vincent Janssen. Our Dutch striker was then on target to make it 5-1 before Shayon Harrison sealed a very impressive win.

Spurs:
Vorm (Lloris 46), Walker (Trippier 46), Alderweireld, Carter-Vickers, Rose (Davies 46); Mason (Winks 46), Dier (Amos 85); Lamela (Edwards 81), Alli (Harrison 76), Eriksen (Janssen 46); Kane (Carroll 62). Substitutes (not used): McGee, Walkes, Wimmer.

I LOVE ERIC DIER... ERIC DIER LOVES ME

Eric Dier didn't take long to earn his Spurs after putting pen to paper at White Hart Lane.

The defensive midfielder swapped Lisbon for London in the summer of 2014 and quickly made his mark after arriving from Sporting.

Supporters didn't have to wait long to see why the Club had pursued the talented player, Dier earning instant hero status with a goal against West Ham United on the opening day of the 2014/2015 campaign.

His superb strike secured a dramatic 1-0 victory for his new team and when he followed that up with a goal on his home debut in a 4-0 win against Queens Park Rangers the following week, he had ensured his Tottenham Hotspur career was off to the best possible start.

Dier became a familiar sight in the Spurs' rearguard, going on to start all but one of his side's Premier League games that season, suspension having ruled him out of a game against Liverpool.

Club progress was soon followed by international success for the man born in Cheltenham but brought up in Portugal.

Having been capped by England at Under-18, Under-19 and Under-20 levels - he also earned nine Under-21 caps – it seemed only a matter of time before he broke through into the senior international set-up.

His impressive domestic form had understandably caught the attention of Roy Hodgson and Dier's rise to prominence was complete when he won his first full cap for England against Spain in November 2015.

The step up in class didn't faze the former Sporting Lisbon Academy graduate, in fact it seemed to spur the player on with Dier opening his England account in stunning fashion.

Just three games into his international career, he was the toast of the nation when he powered home a dramatic stoppage-time header to defeat hosts Germany 3-2 in the Olympiastadion in Berlin – Tottenham team-mate Harry Kane and Leicester's Jamie Vardy the other scorers in a pulsating encounter.

The versatile White Hart Lane star is established in the role of defensive midfielder for club and country – he started 50 of 53 games in all competitions for Spurs last season and played all four matches for England at Euro 2016.

His highlight in Euro 2016 was the free-kick he scored against Russia, his country's first goal in the group stages.

Dier later revealed that he had spent a lot of his time growing up practising such accuracy from dead-ball situations.

Sporting Lisbon's loss has most certainly been Tottenham Hotspur's gain.

Opta stat: 8 - Eric Dier was the 8th Tottenham Hotspur player to score for England at a major tournament, more than any other club.

"He's got it all in that position. He has to be one of the first names on the teamsheet now and that's how important he is to Spurs and the England set-up." Ledley King on Eric Dier

GOAL OF THE SEASON 2015/2016

Thousands of you took the time to vote on tottenhamhotspur.com and via @SpursOfficial. Here's the top 10:

10. Harry Kane vs Chelsea (2 May 2016) – 2%
9. Dele Alli vs Leicester City (22 August 2015) – 5.2%
8. Heung-Min Son vs Watford (28 December 2015) – 4.5%
7. Mousa Dembélé vs Anderlecht (5 November 2015) – 3.9%
6. Christian Eriksen vs Manchester City (14 February 2016) – 3.8%
5. Christian Eriksen, second goal vs Swansea City (4 October 2015) – 2.7%
4. Ryan Mason vs Sunderland (13 September 2015) – 2%
3. Harry Kane, first goal vs Stoke City (18 April 2016) – 2%
2. Harry Kane vs Arsenal (5 March 2016) – 21.3%

And the winner is…

With a whopping 52.6% of the vote, Dele Alli's incredible strike in the 3-1 win at Crystal Palace in January 2016. It was very much an 'I was there' moment, a goal where the home supporters reluctantly applaud, and one you enjoy watching over and over again. With the score finely poised at 1-1, and just over six minutes remaining at Selhurst Park, Harry Kane whipped the ball out to the left side for Christian Eriksen, who controlled it with his head straight into Dele's path 20 yards from goal. What followed was truly sublime. The midfielder took a touch, flicked the ball over his (and Mile Jedinak's) head, turned and struck a low right-footed shot into the net. Dele's goal was also selected as Match of the Day's Goal of the Season.

Dele said:

"It was a bit of a natural thing. I didn't really think about it too much and I sort of shocked myself – I think you could tell from my celebration, I didn't really know what to do."

Let's not forget…

Harry Kane's stunner against Arsenal in March 2016. A long ball down the left flank looked like it was heading out for a goal-kick, but Dele Alli chased it down and back-heeled the ball into the path of the supporting Kane, who moved into the area and sent a stunning, curling drive into the far top corner of David Ospina's net from a tight angle.

GUESS THE PLAYER

Can you guess the current or former Spurs star with the four clues provided? No cheating!

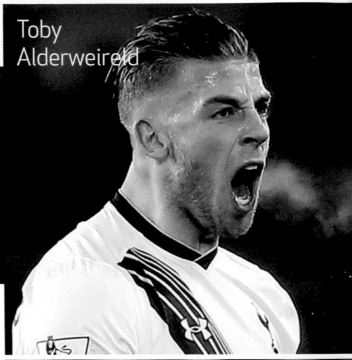

Toby Alderweireld

a. I'm a former German international
b. I also played for Leicester City
c. I've also represented Spurs as an Assistant Head Coach
d. I was a crowd favourite!

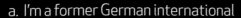

a. I'm an England international
b. I scored 10 league goals last season
c. I made my Premier League debut last season
d. I like to wave a lot!

Steffen Freund

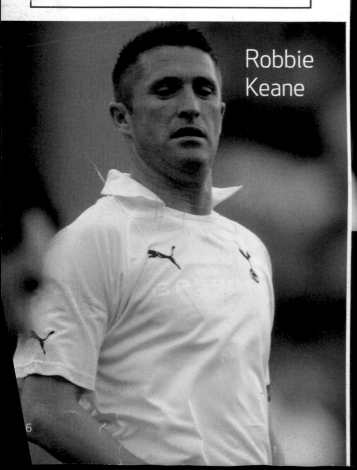

Robbie Keane

a. I joined Spurs from Fulham
b. I'm in my fifth season at the Club
c. I started my career at Beerschot AC
d. I scored on my Spurs debut

a. I'm in my second season at Spurs

b. I scored at Euro 2016

c. I've also played in Holland and Spain

d. I featured in every Premier League match last season

Kyle Walker

a. I joined Spurs in 2003

b. I captained my club and my country

c. I now live in Los Angeles

d. I'm a striker

Dele Alli

Mousa Dembélé

a. I'm in my eighth season at Spurs

b. I represented my country at Euro 2016

c. I was born in 1990

d. I've had loan spells at Aston Villa, QPR & Northampton

Answers on p.60-61

p.48 Super Spurs Quiz

1. Everton
2. Dele Alli
3. Kenya
4. CSKA Moscow, Bayer Leverkusen and AS Monaco
5. 61,000
6. 25
7. Jan Vertonghen, Toby Alderweireld & Mousa Dembélé
8. Eric Dier
9. True
10. Four
11. Manchester United
12. Gary Mabbutt
13. Christian Eriksen
14. Sheffield United

p.37 Word Search

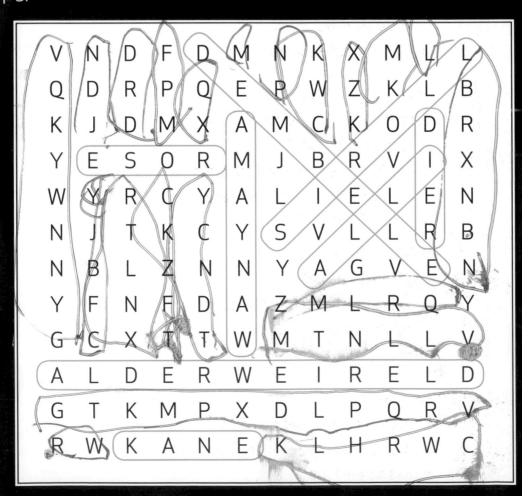

V	N	D	F	D	M	N	K	X	M	L	L
Q	D	R	P	Q	E	P	W	Z	K	L	B
K	J	D	M	X	A	M	C	K	O	D	R
Y	E	S	O	R	M	J	B	R	V	I	X
W	Y	R	C	Y	A	L	I	E	L	E	N
N	J	T	K	C	Y	S	V	L	L	R	B
N	B	L	Z	N	N	Y	A	G	V	E	N
Y	F	F	N	F	D	A	Z	M	L	R	Q	Y
G	C	X	T	T	W	M	T	N	L	L	V
A	L	D	E	R	W	E	I	R	E	L	D
G	T	K	M	P	X	D	L	P	Q	R	V
R	W	K	A	N	E	K	L	H	R	W	C

p.56-57 Guess the Player Answers

Mousa Dembélé

a. I joined Spurs from Fulham

b. I'm in my fifth season at the Club

c. I started my career at Beerschot AC

d. I scored on my Spurs debut

Dele Alli

a. I'm an England international

b. I scored 10 league goals last season

c. I made my Premier League debut last season

d. I like to wave a lot!

Steffen Freund

a. I'm a former German international

b. I also played for Leicester City

c. I've also represented Spurs as an Assistant Head Coach

d. I was a crowd favourite!

Toby Alderweireld

a. I'm in my second season at Spurs

b. I scored at Euro 2016

c. I've also played in Holland and Spain

d. I featured in every Premier League match last season

Robbie Keane

a. I joined Spurs in 2003

b. I captained my club and my country

c. I now live in Los Angeles

d. I'm a striker

Kyle Walker

a. I'm in my eighth season at Spurs

b. I represented my country at Euro 2016

c. I was born in 1990

d. I've had loan spells at Aston Villa, QPR & Northampton